SCHOLASTIC

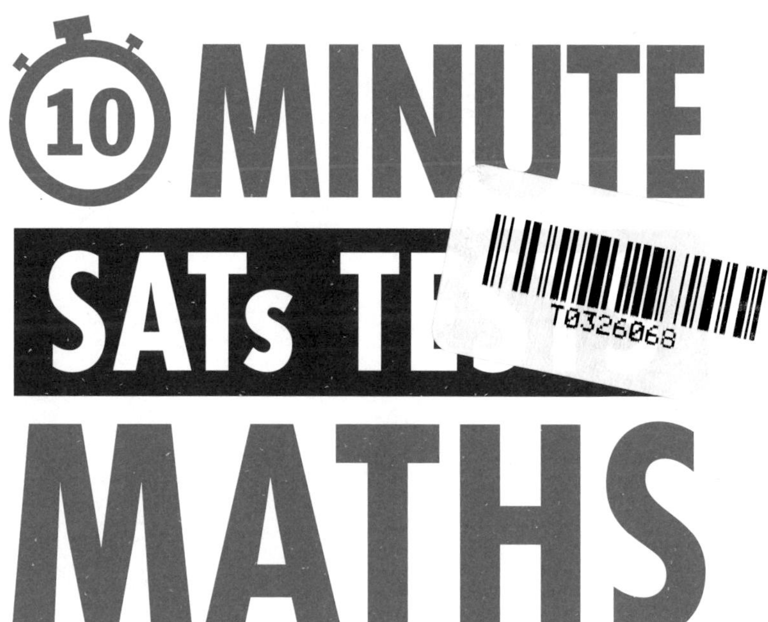

AGES 7–8
YEAR 3

KS2

Scholastic Education, an imprint of Scholastic Ltd
Book End, Range Road, Witney, Oxfordshire, OX29 0YD
Registered office: Westfield Road, Southam, Warwickshire CV47 0RA
www.scholastic.co.uk

© 2018, Scholastic Ltd

2 3 4 5 6 7 8 9 8 9 0 1 2 3 4 5 6 7
British Library Cataloguing-in-Publication Data
A catalogue record for this book is available from the British Library.

ISBN 978-1407-17524-9

Printed and bound by Bell and Bain Ltd, Glasgow

All rights reserved. This book is sold subject to the condition that it shall not, by way of trade or otherwise, be lent, hired out or otherwise circulated without the publisher's prior consent in any form of binding or cover other than that in which it is published and without a similar condition, including this condition, being imposed upon the subsequent purchaser.

No part of this publication may be reproduced, stored in a retrieval system, or transmitted, in any form or by any means, electronic, mechanical, photocopying, recording or otherwise, other than for the purposes described in the content of this product, without the prior permission of the publisher. This product remains in copyright. Every effort has been made to trace copyright holders for the works reproduced in this book, and the publishers apologise for any inadvertent omissions.

Author
Paul Hollin

Editorial team
Rachel Morgan, Audrey Stokes, Kate Baxter, Sarah Chappelow

Series Design
Scholastic Design Team: Nicolle Thomas and Neil Salt

Design
Claire Green

Cover Design
Scholastic Design Team: Nicolle Thomas and Neil Salt

Cover Illustration
Adam Linley

Illustrations
Technical Artwork: Dave Morris
Figures: Carys Evans

Contents

How to use this book

This book contains four different sets of maths tests for Year 3, each containing SATs-style questions. Each set comprises one arithmetic test followed by two reasoning tests. As a whole, the complete set of tests provides full coverage of the test framework for this age group, across the two strands of the maths curriculum: Number; and Measurement, geometry and statistics.

Some questions require a selected response, for example where children choose the correct answer from several options. Other questions require a constructed response, where children work out and write down their own answer.

A mark scheme, skills check and progress chart are also included towards the end of this book.

Completing the tests

- It is intended that children will take approximately ten minutes to complete each individual test; or approximately 30 minutes to complete each set of three tests.
- After your child has completed each set, mark the tests and together identify and practise any areas where your child is less confident. Ask them to complete the next set at a later date, when you feel they have had enough time to practise and improve.

Set A

Test 1: Arithmetic

Marks

1. $3 \times 5 =$

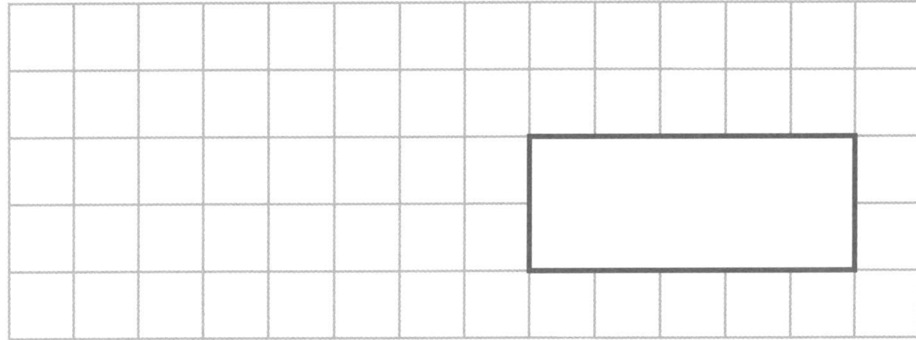

1

2. $15 + 22 =$

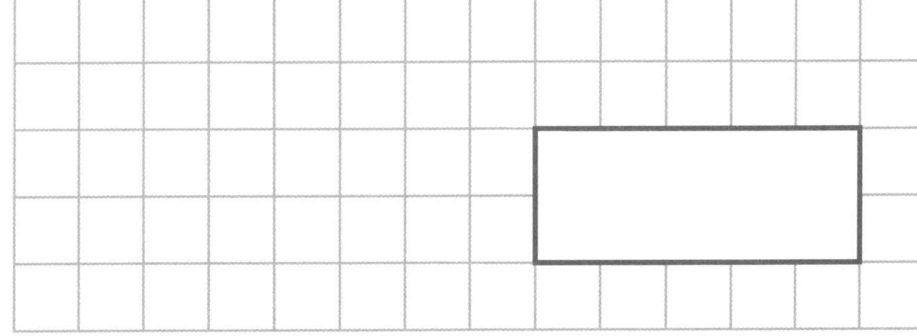

1

3. $\frac{1}{10} + \frac{1}{10} + \frac{1}{10} + \frac{1}{10} =$

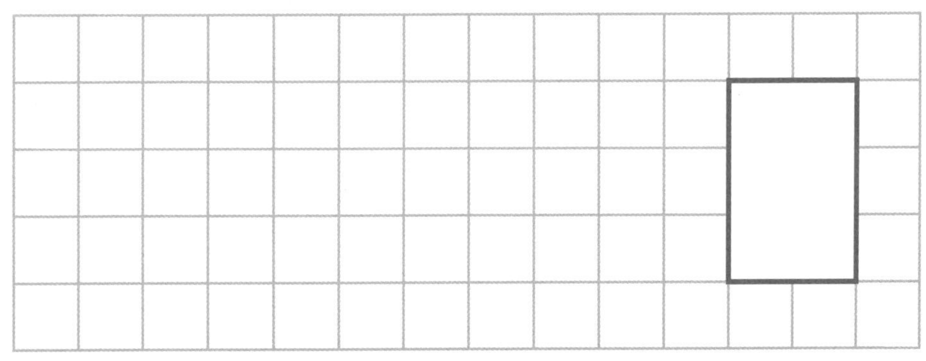

1

Marks

4. $250 \div 5 =$

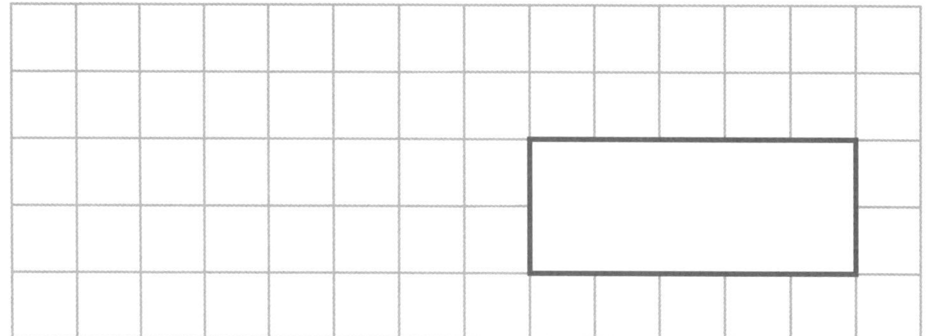

1

5. $100 + 100 + 100 + 100 =$

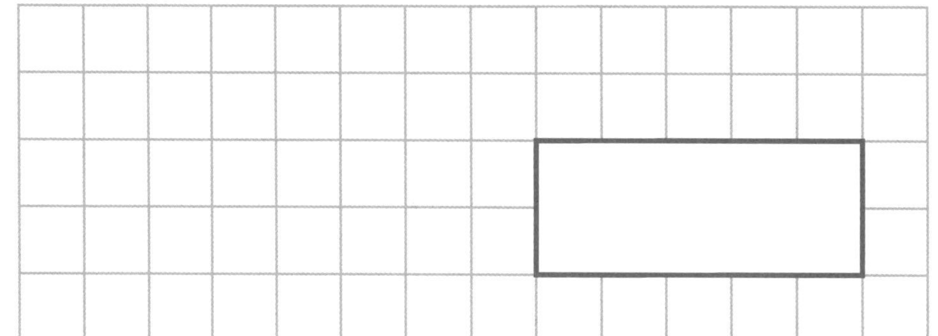

1

6. $\frac{4}{5} - \frac{3}{5} =$

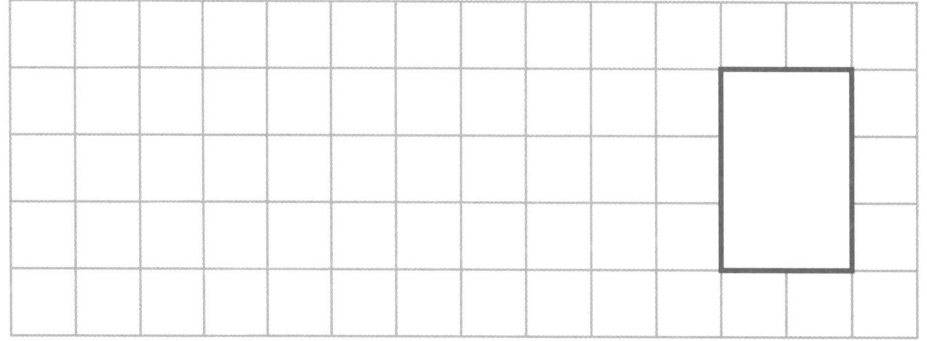

1

Marks

7. 394 + 217 =

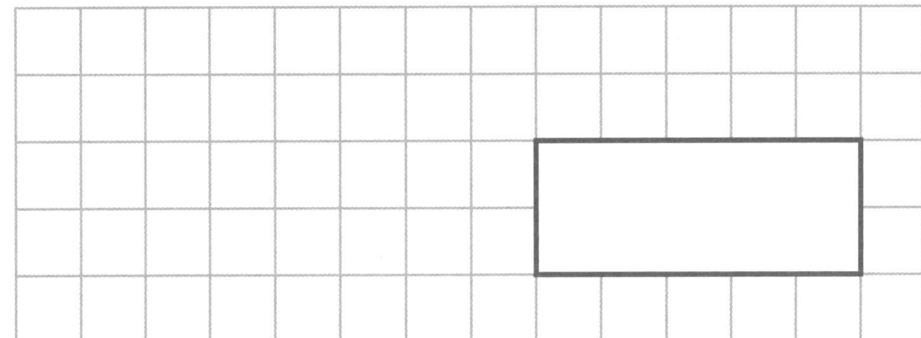

1

8.  × 9 = 72

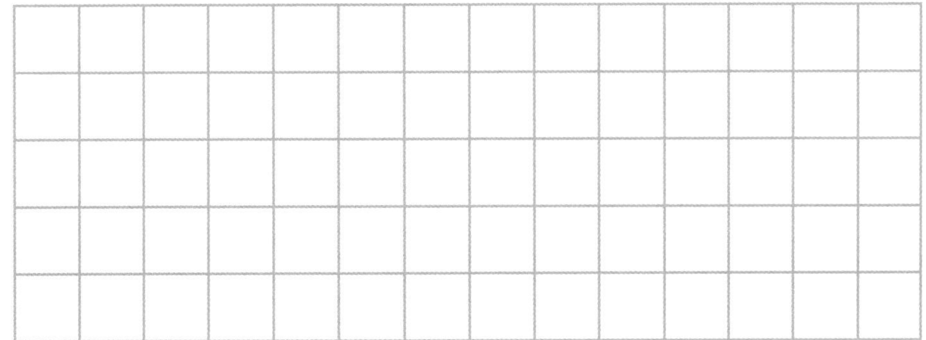

1

9.

547 − 111 =

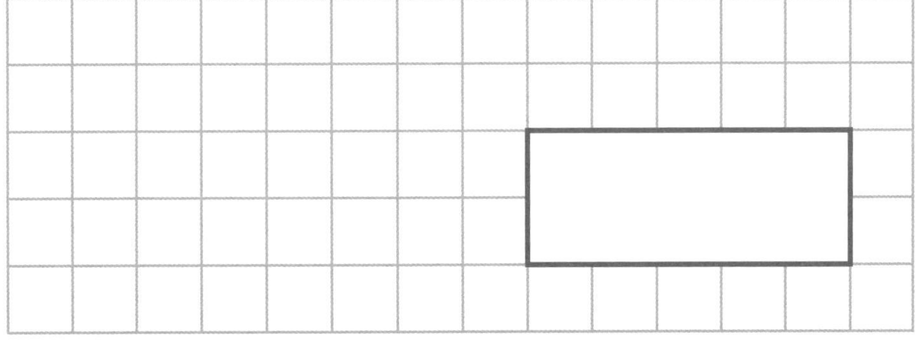

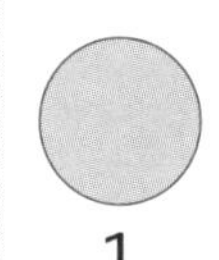

1

Marks

10.

Show your method

		2	5	4
	×			3

2

Well done! END OF SET A TEST 1!

Set A

Test 2: Reasoning

Marks

1. Complete this grid. The first one is done for you.

62	sixty-two
145	
	six hundred and eighty-three
904	

1

2.

Fraction of pizza	Price
$\frac{1}{4}$	50p
$\frac{1}{3}$	70p
$\frac{1}{2}$	90p

A pizza stall sells different-size slices of pizza.

Write the correct price under each slice.

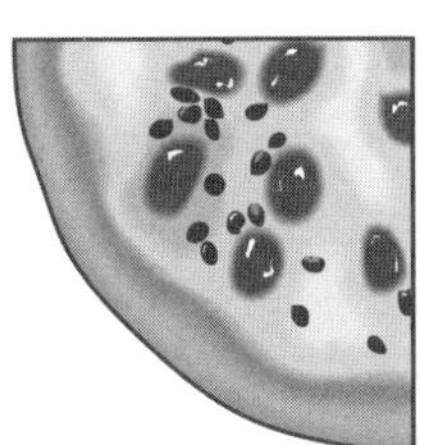

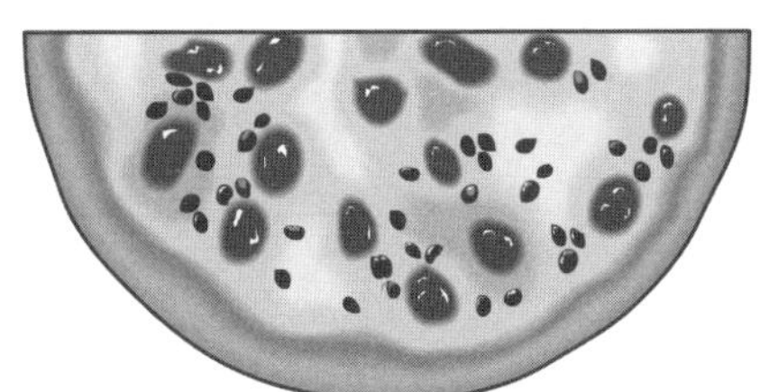

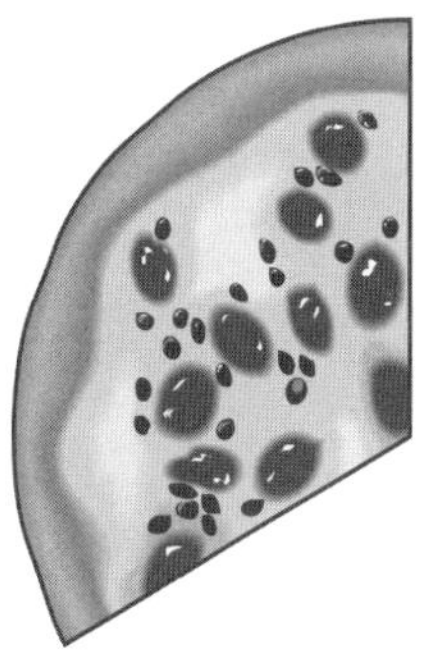

_______ p _______ p _______ p

1

Marks

3. Circle the best estimate for this addition.

238 + 325 + 400

900 950 1000 1050

1

4. Jenna describes a shape:

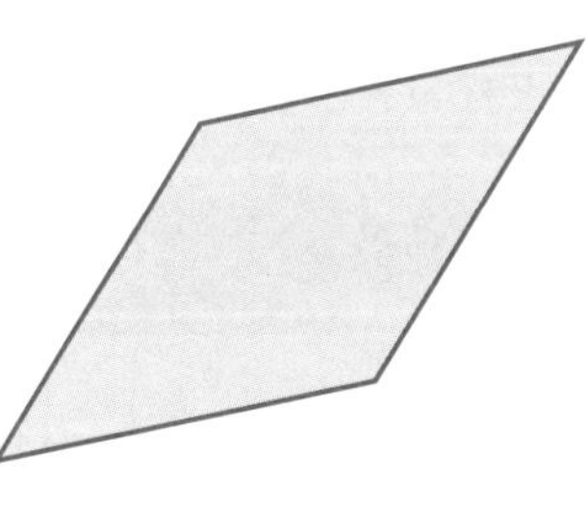

It has four equal length sides, two equal obtuse angles opposite each other, and two equal acute angles opposite each other. It is a...

a. Name Jenna's shape:

____

1

b. Name and describe this shape:

____

____

____

____

1

Marks

5. Dimitri buys a pen and a pencil. He gives the shop assistant a £5 note.

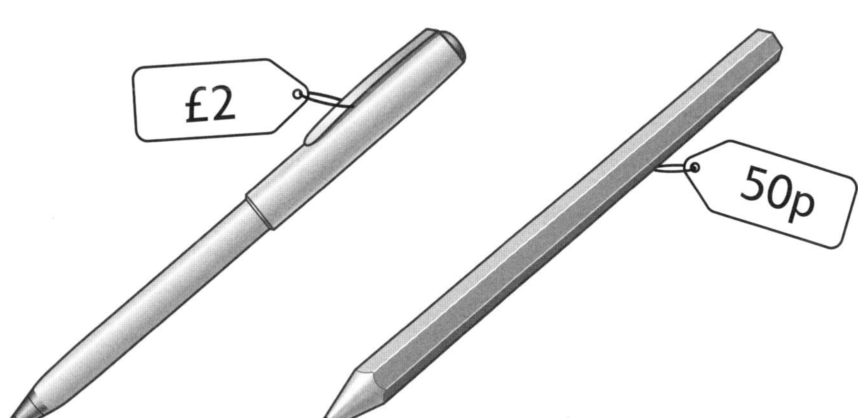

How much change will he receive?

He will receive £ [ ] and [ ] p change

1

Circle the coins he might receive for his change.

1

Marks

6. Tina collects stickers in a book.

There is space for 8 stickers on each page, and there are 12 pages in the book.

Tina needs 13 more stickers to complete her book and claim her prize.

How many stickers has she already collected?

Show your method

______ stickers

2

Well done! END OF SET A TEST 2!

Set A

Test 3: Reasoning

Marks

1. Circle $\frac{1}{4}$ of these beads.

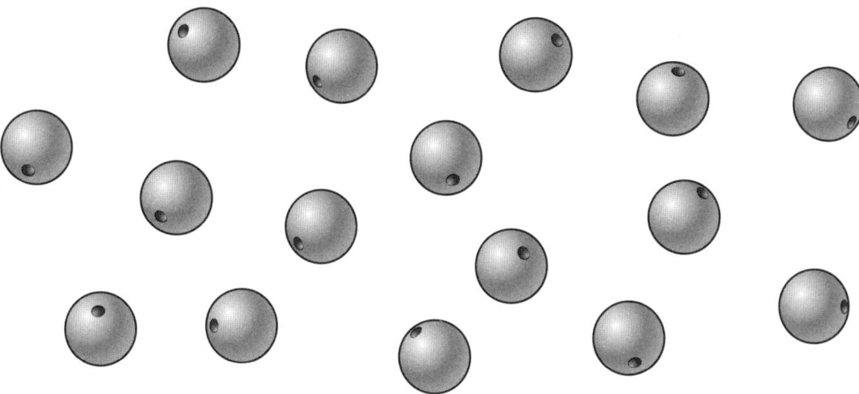

1

2. Alonso starts school at 9.30am. Lunch starts 3 hours later.

On the first clock, draw the time that lunch starts.

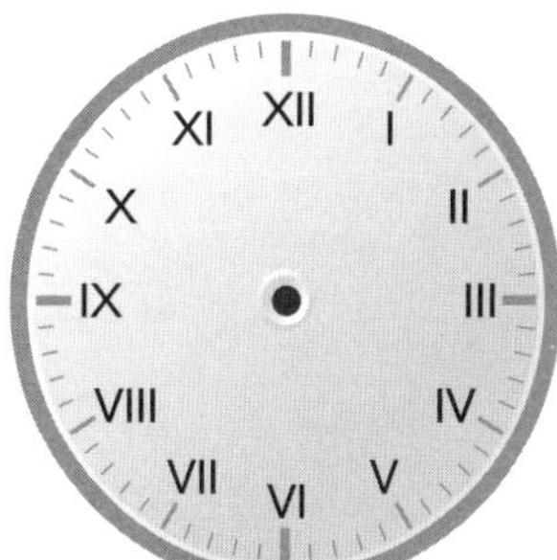

Alonso finishes school at 3.45pm, and arrives home half an hour later.

On the second clock, draw the time he gets home.

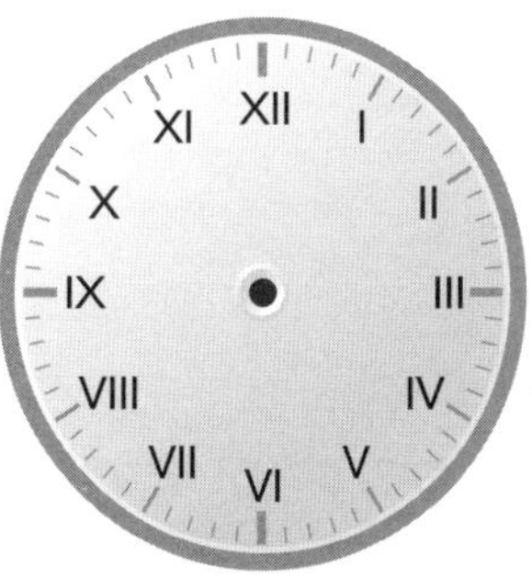

1

3. Look at this rectangle. Draw another rectangle that is exactly four times bigger.

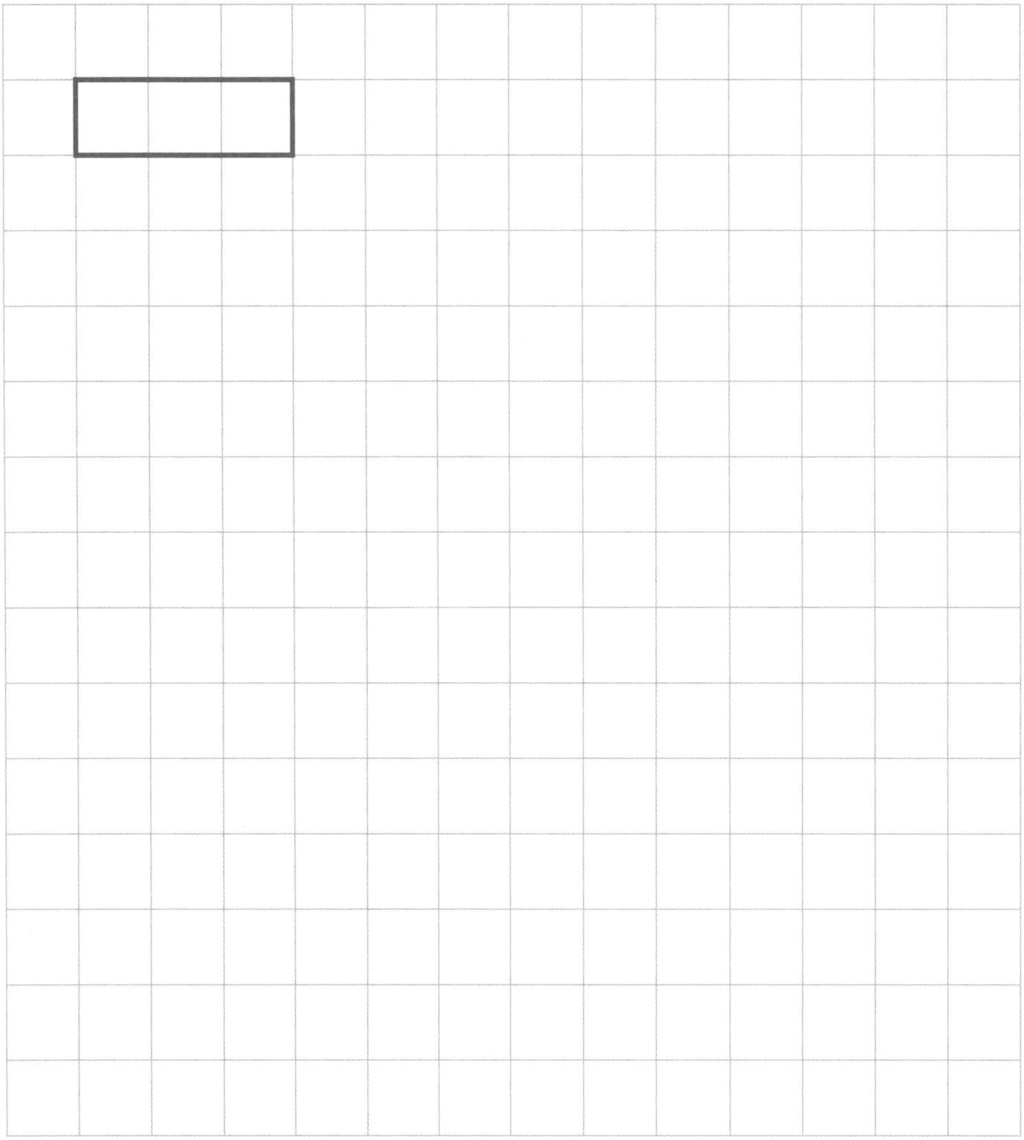

1

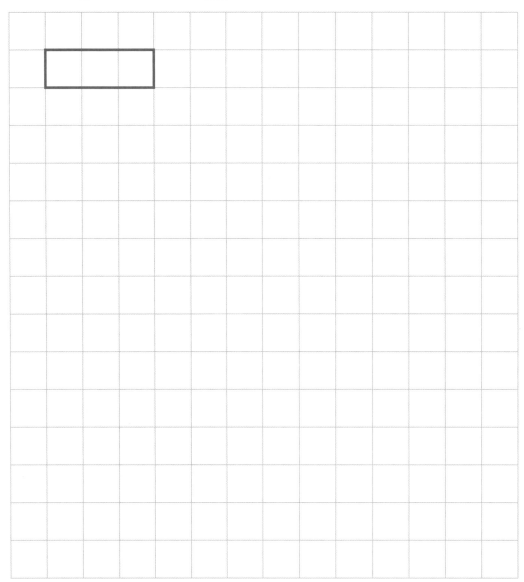

What is the perimeter of your rectangle? cm

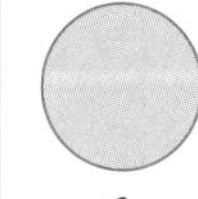

1

Marks

4. Jen writes a sequence:

0 110 220 330 440 550 660

What is the rule for her sequence?

____

____

1

5. This bar of chocolate is divided between five people.

Kiki gets $\frac{1}{2}$ of the whole bar.

Lorenzo gets $\frac{1}{4}$ of the whole bar.

Amelie, Jake and Bruno each get the same amount.

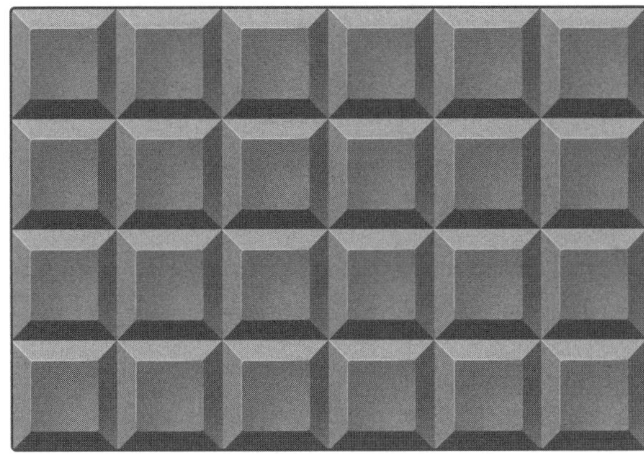

How many squares of chocolate will Amelie, Jake and Bruno each get?

[ ] squares each

1

Marks

6. The bar chart shows how many hours of sunshine there were each day of a week.

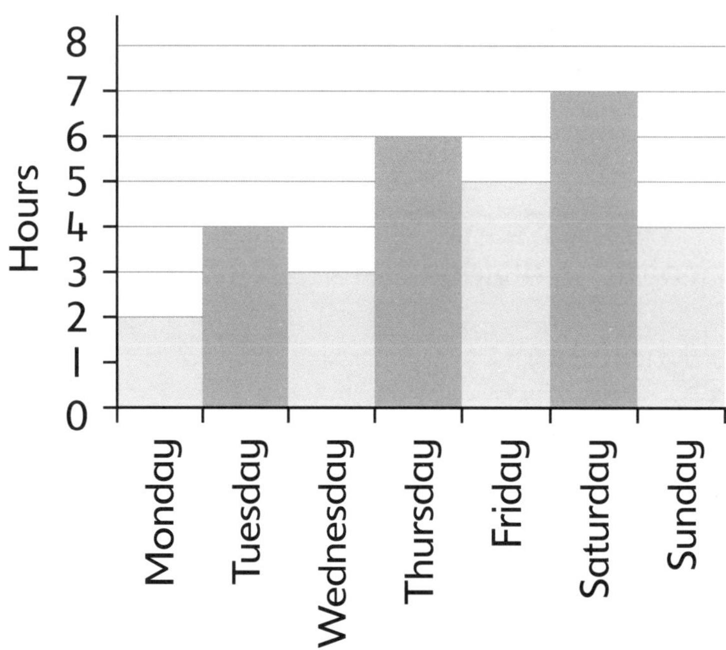

How many more hours of sunshine were there on the sunniest day than on the least sunny day?

1

Which two days, combined, had the same amount of sunshine as Friday?

1

Well done! END OF SET A TEST 3!

Set B

Test 1: Arithmetic

Marks

1. $\frac{1}{10} + \frac{1}{10} + \frac{1}{10} =$

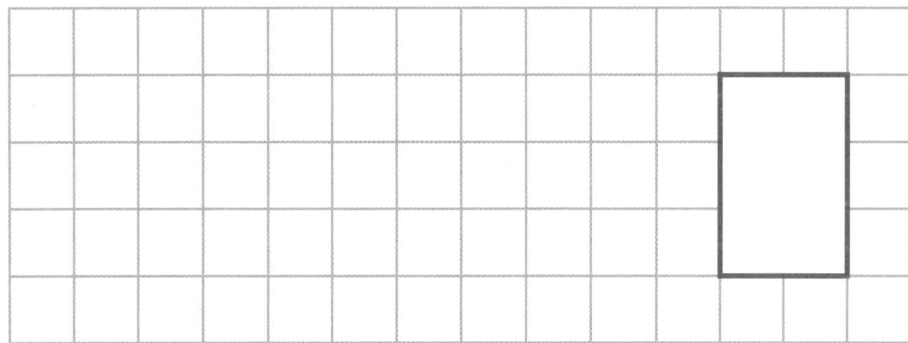

1

2. $3 \times 12 =$

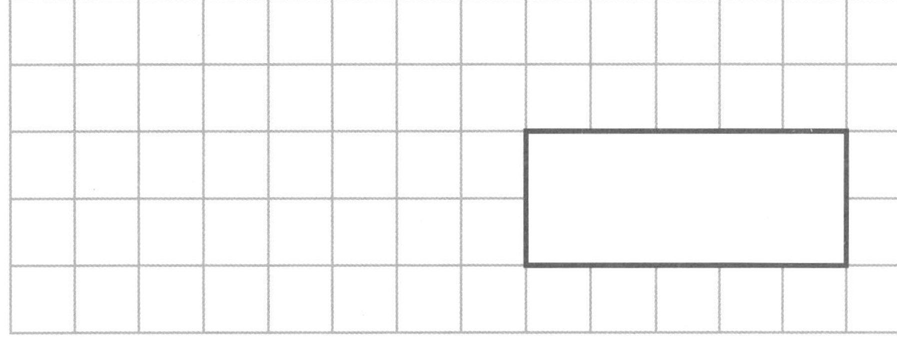

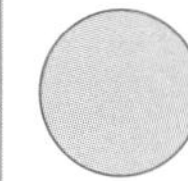

1

3. $4 + 4 + 4 + 4 + 4 =$

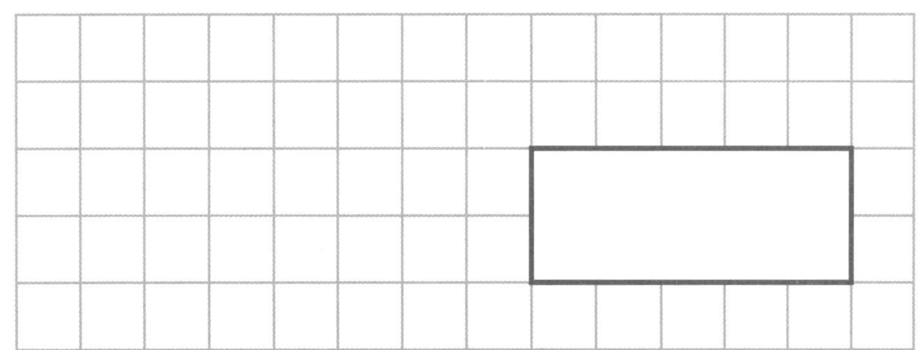

1

Marks

4. 74 − ☐ = 68

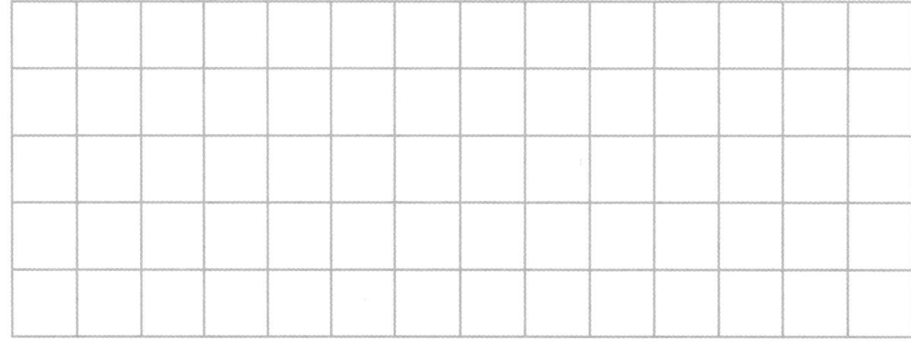

1

5. 21 × 5 =

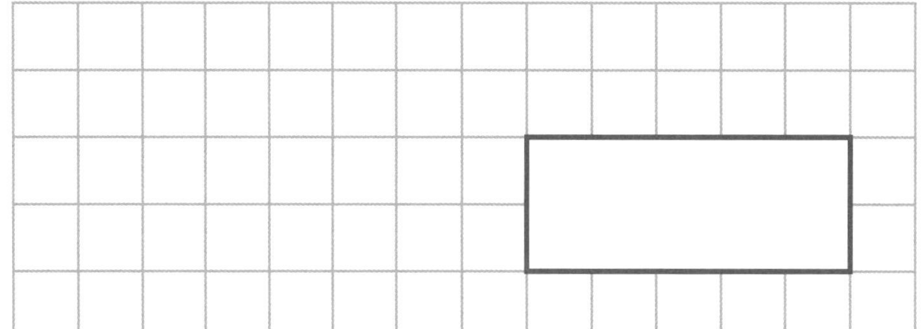

1

6. 159 + 300 =

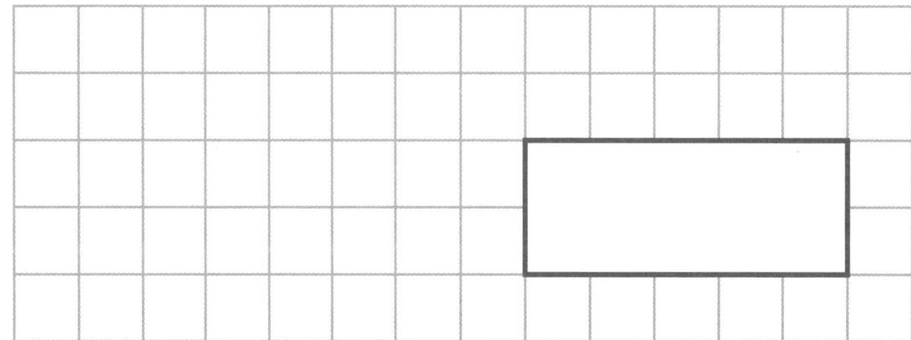

1

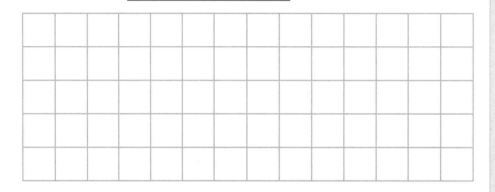

Marks

7. $\frac{4}{7} + \frac{2}{7} =$

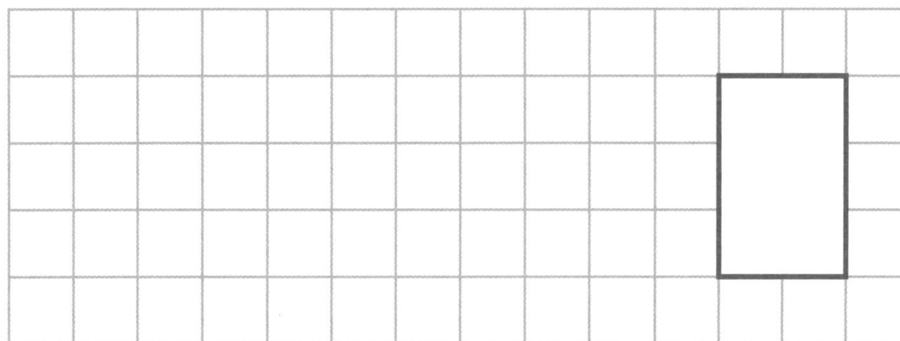

1

8. $80 \div 4 =$

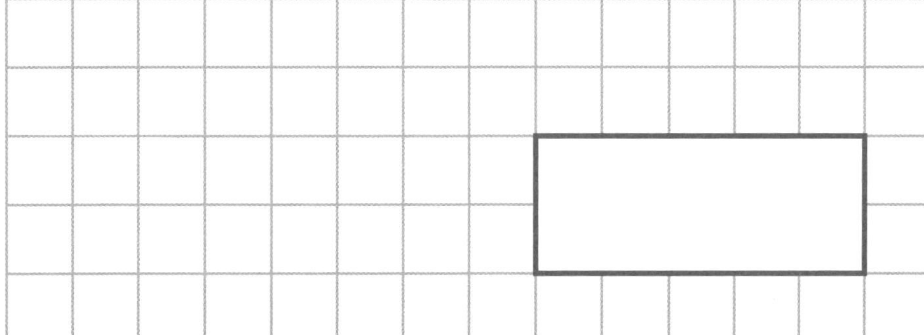

1

9. $731 - 317 =$

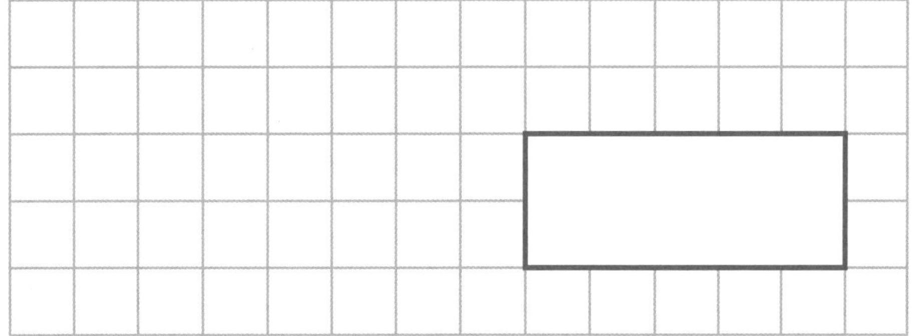

1

Set B

Test 1: Arithmetic

10.

Show your method

		1	5	2
	×			6

Marks

2

Well done! END OF SET B TEST 1!

Set B

Test 2: Reasoning

Marks

1. Complete the chart by rounding the number given to the nearest ten, and to the nearest 100. One has been done for you.

Rounded to the nearest 10	Number	Rounded to the nearest 100
410	412	400
	287	
	647	

1

2. Write each of these fractions in the correct place on the number line.

$\frac{1}{2}$ $\frac{1}{5}$ $\frac{3}{4}$ $\frac{1}{3}$

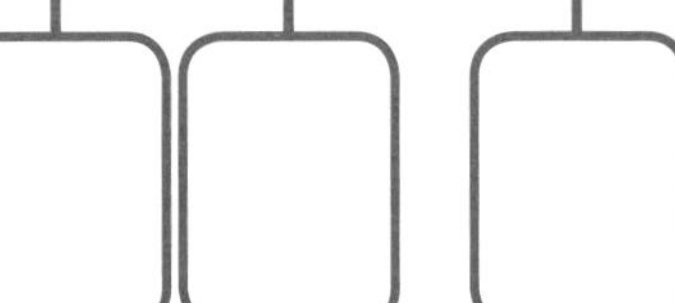
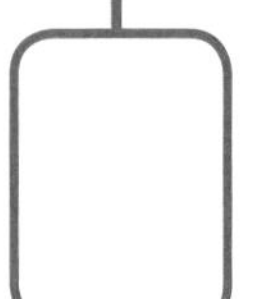

0 1

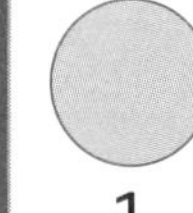

1

Marks

3. Samir started to draw a regular polygon on this grid.
Use a pencil and ruler to complete Samir's drawing.

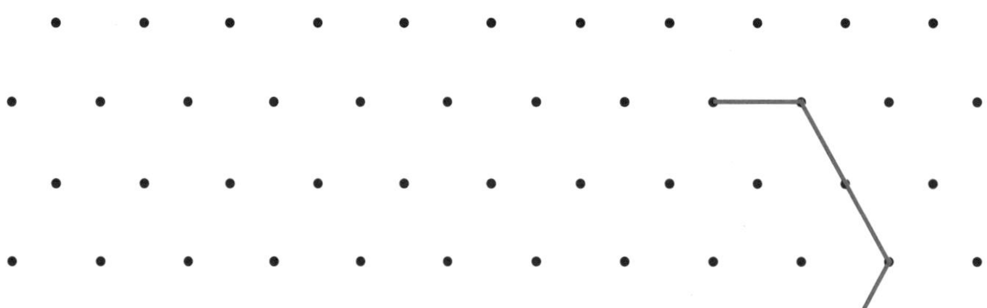

1

Name the shape. ______________________________

1

4. Joanna says:

Write an inverse number statement to prove that she is right.

1

Marks

5. A class are learning about poetry.

The teacher only has nine poetry books, and she wants the children to work in pairs, each pair sharing a book.

If there are 32 children in the class, how many **more** books will be needed?

Show your method

more books

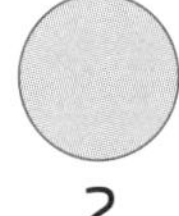

2

Marks

6. Sam is pouring drinks at his party.

He has a jug with 1 litre of squash in it. He needs to fill eleven 80ml cups.

How much squash will be left over after he has filled the cups?

Show your method

ml

2

Well done! END OF SET B TEST 2!

Set B

Test 3: Reasoning

Marks

1. This is a plan of a minibus with 12 seats.

Half of the seats have passengers in them.
These are the ones with a cross on them.

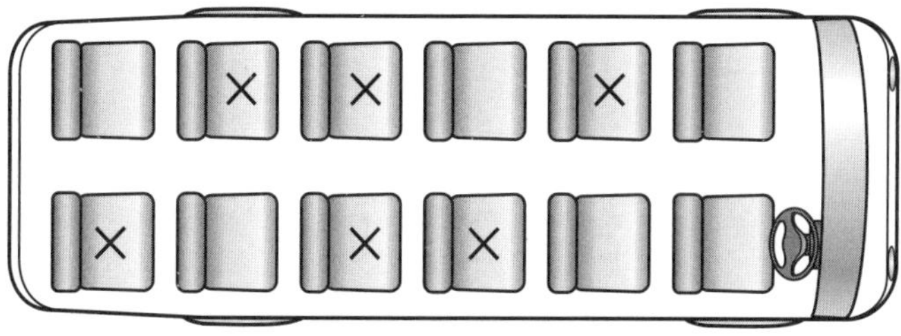

Draw crosses to show each of these fractions of passengers on the coach plans below.

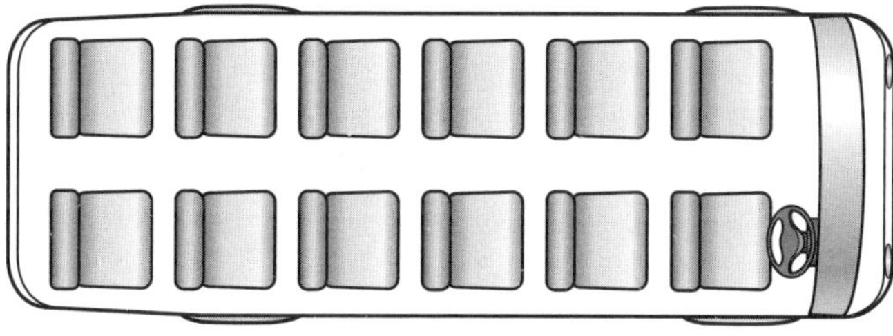

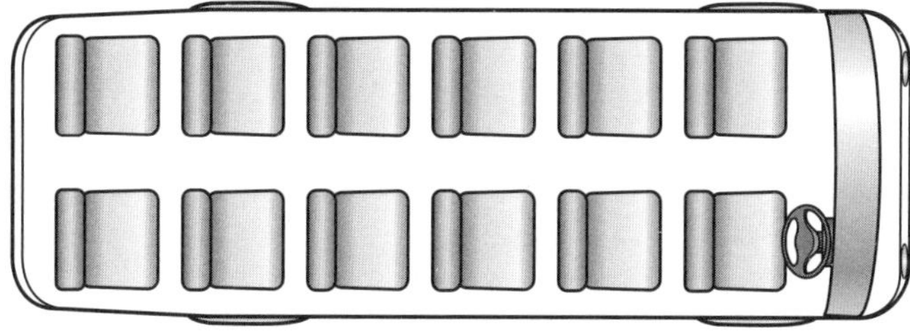

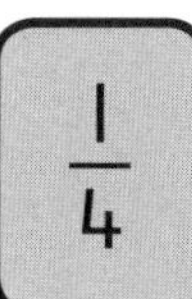

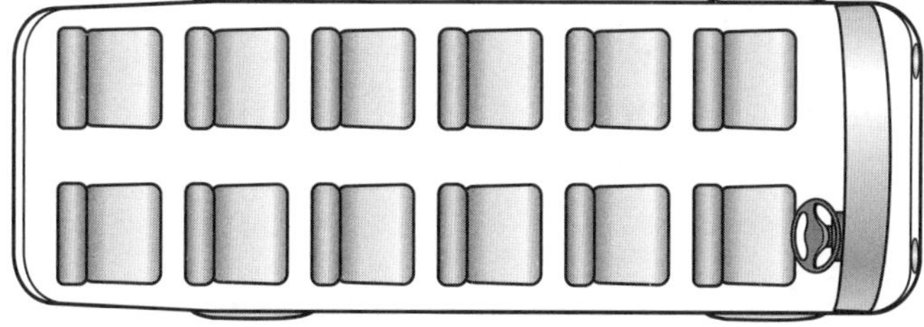

1

Marks

2. Write the missing digits to complete this addition.

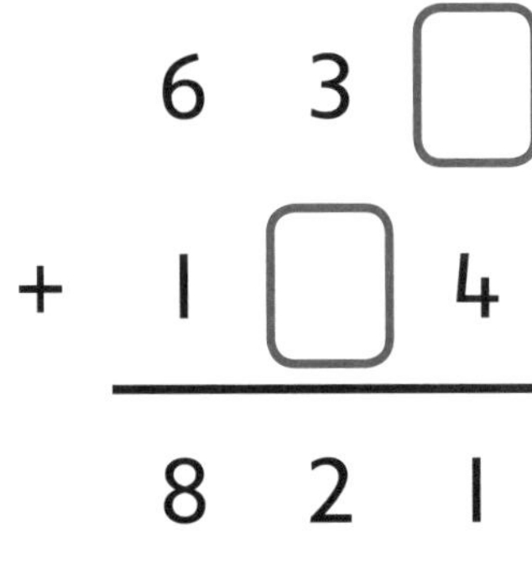

1

3. These times show what happens in the morning at a school.

School starts	Break starts	Break ends	Lunchtime starts

How long is it from when school starts until lunchtime begins?

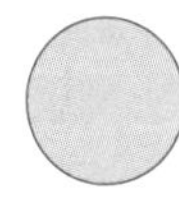

1

The lesson from school starting until break starts is longer than the lesson between break and lunchtime.

How much longer?

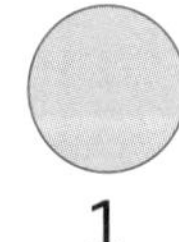

1

4. Which of these types of line does this shape have?

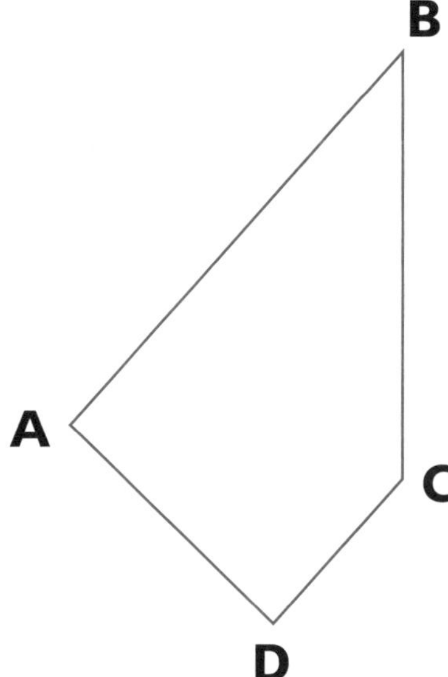

Put a tick in each correct box.

- ☐ Parallel line
- ☐ Perpendicular line
- ☐ Horizontal line
- ☐ Vertical line

1

Write the name of each angle. One has been done for you.

A 

B

C

D

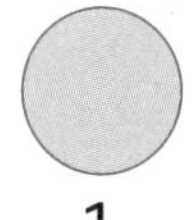
1

Marks

5. Altogether, there are 564 children in a primary school.

One day, all the children in Year 3 go on a school trip to the seaside.

On the same day there are 5 children from Year 4 who are absent from school.

If there are 489 children still in school that day, calculate how many children have gone on the school trip.

Show your method

children

2

Well done! END OF SET B TEST 3!

Set C

Test 1: Arithmetic

Marks

1. 12 ÷ 3 =

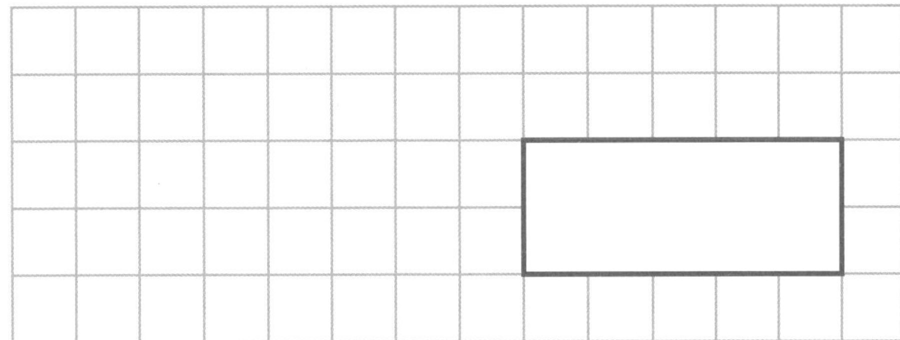

1

2. 200 + 500 =

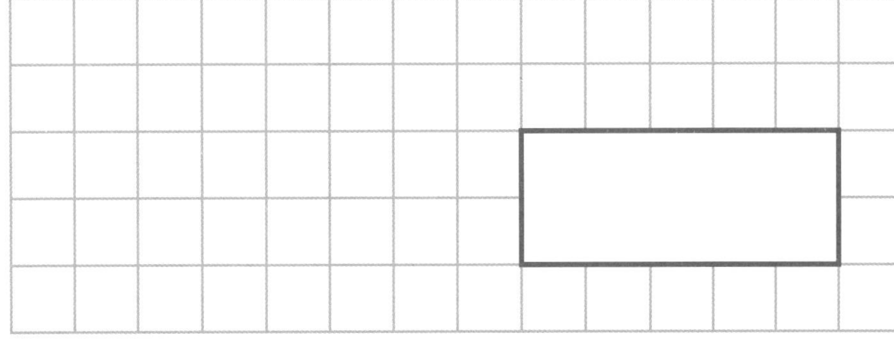

1

3. 5 + 5 + 5 + 5 =

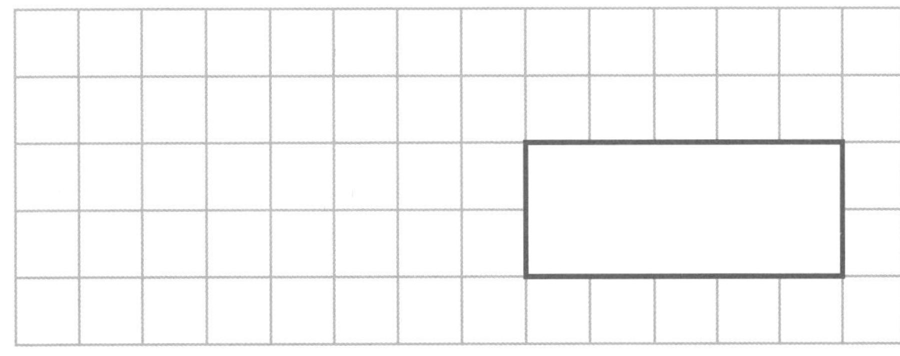

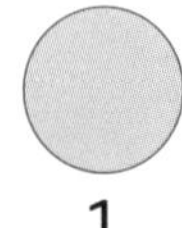

1

Marks

4. $\frac{1}{10} + \frac{1}{10} + \frac{1}{10} =$

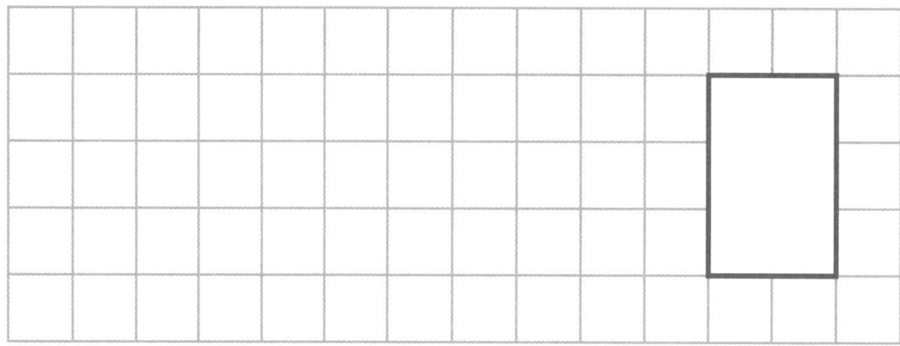

1

5.  × 6 = 36

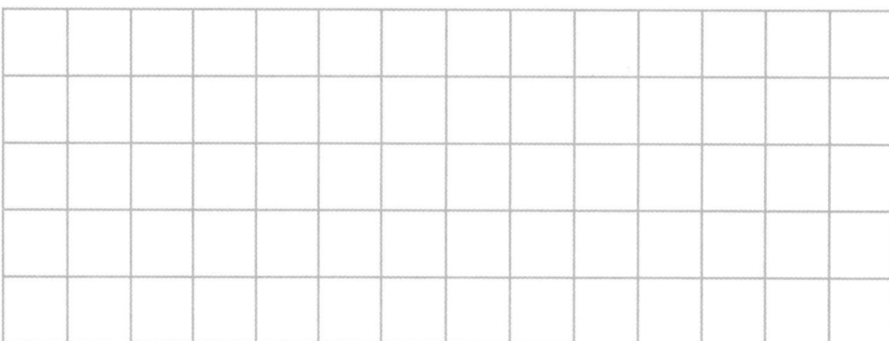

1

Marks

6. $195 - 90 =$

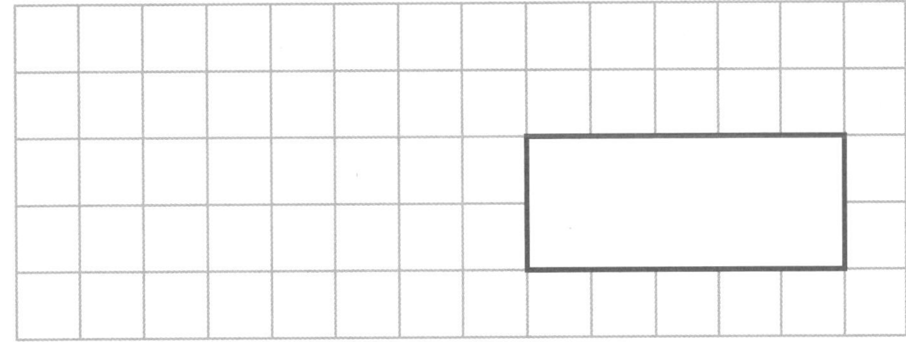

1

7. $\frac{5}{8} - \frac{2}{8} =$

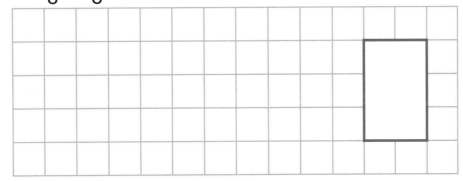

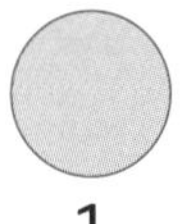

1

8. $120 \times 3 =$

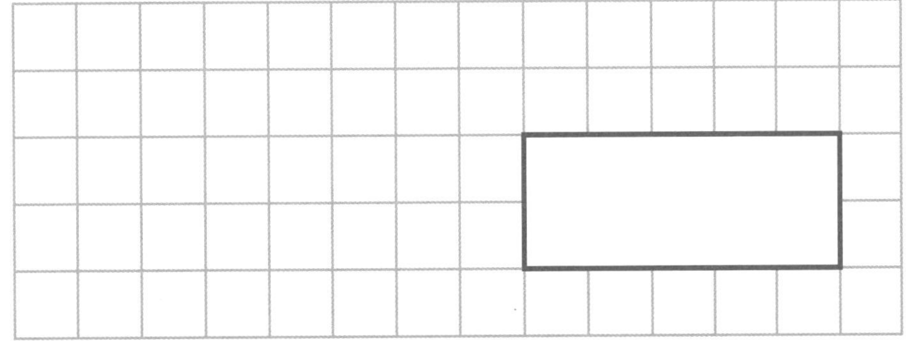

1

Marks

9. 582 + 347 =

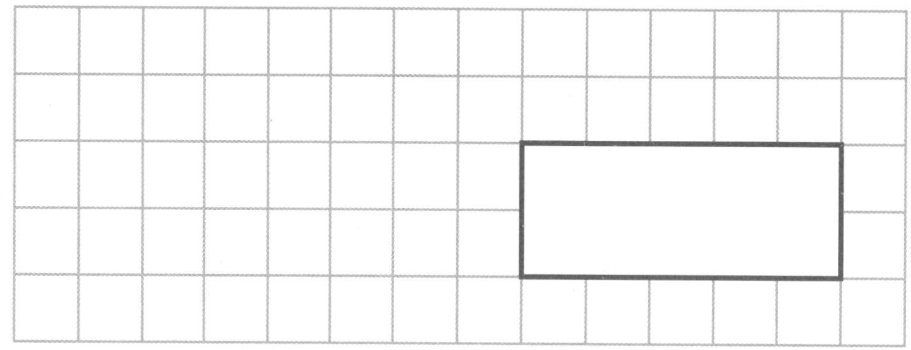

2

10.

Show your method

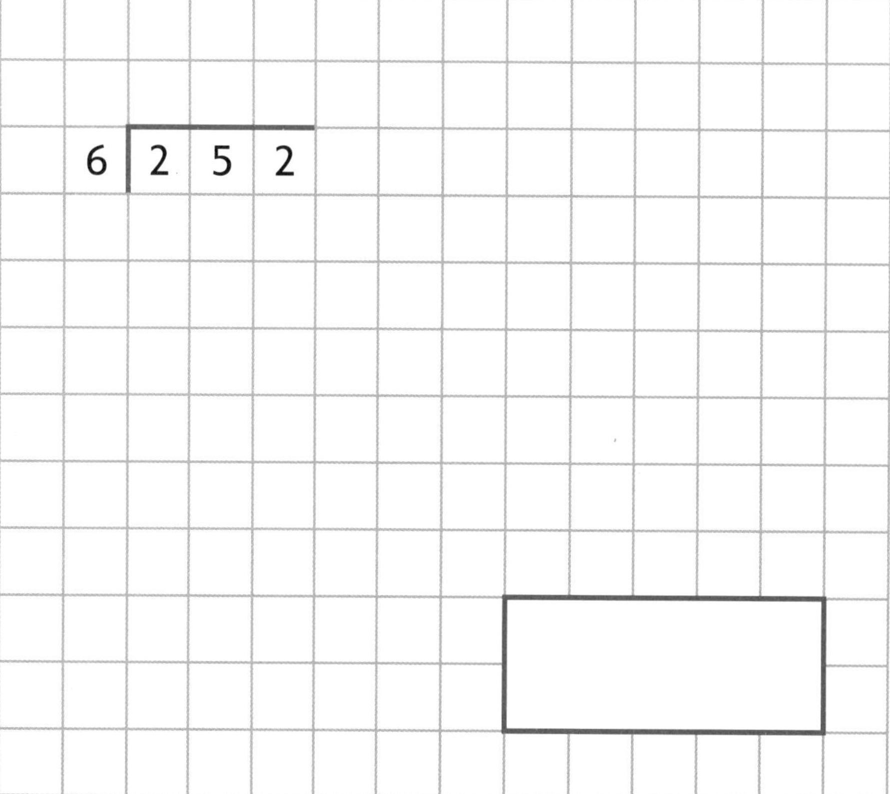

2

Well done! END OF SET C TEST 1!

Set C

Test 2: Reasoning

Marks

1. Use a ruler to find out how much longer line B is than line A.

B

A

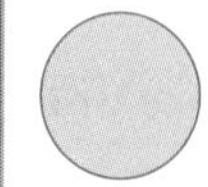

1

2. Write the missing digits to make this multiplication correct.

 6

× 3

7 □

1

Marks

3. Adam makes a sequence using the numbers 1, 2, 3 and 4.

Taking each number in turn, he multiplies it by 2 then adds 1.

This gives him the sequence 3, 5, 7, 9

Next, he creates a new sequence for the numbers 1, 2, 3 and 4.

Taking each number in turn, he multiplies it by 3 then subtracts 1.

Write the next three numbers of the sequence.

2   

1

---

4. A bag contains black beads, grey beads and white beads. What fraction of the beads are grey?

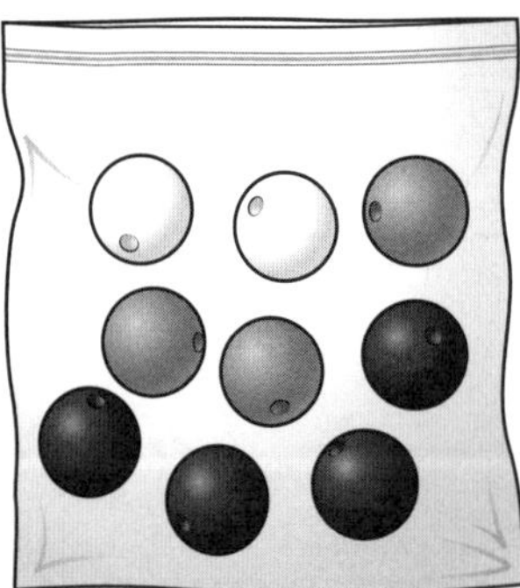

1

Marks

5. There are 1000g in 1kg.

If 100g of berries costs £3, how much would 1kg of berries cost?

£

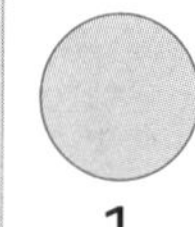

1

If 500g of flour costs £2 and 50p, how much would 1kg of flour cost?

£

1

If 250g of sugar costs £1, how much would 1kg of sugar cost?

£

1

Marks

6. This bar chart shows the results of a class survey of favourite wild animals.

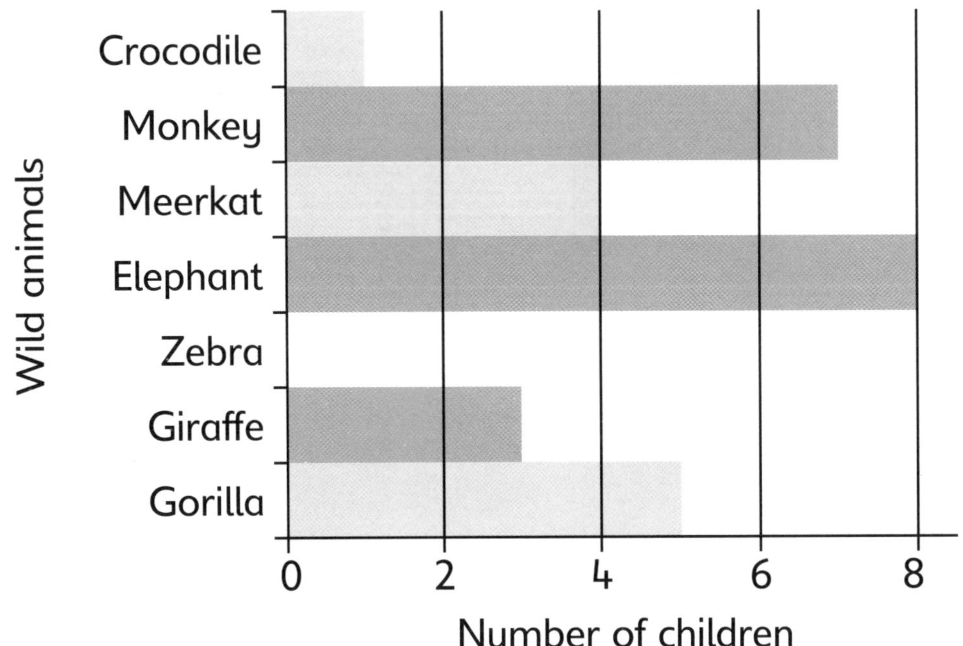

Name the least popular and most popular wild animals.

Least popular: ______________________

Most popular: ______________________

1

How many more children preferred monkeys to giraffes?

[ ] children

1

Well done! END OF SET C TEST 2!

Set C

Test 3: Reasoning

Marks

1. Use these three digits to make a number that can go in the space.

2 4 8

$248 < \square < 842$

1

---

2. Trevone estimates that he weighs 35kg.

Then he weighs himself.

By how many kilograms was he wrong?

1

Trevone's friend Gina weighs 41kg.

Where would the needle point if Trevone and Gina stood on the scales together?

kg

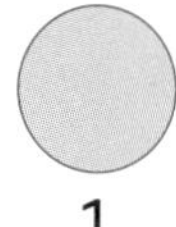
1

Marks

3. Gemma wants to build a tower using three different types of 3D shape.

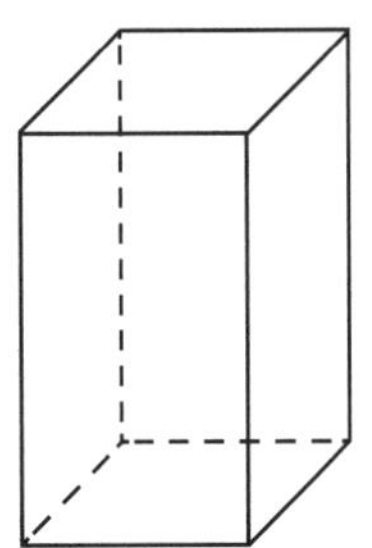
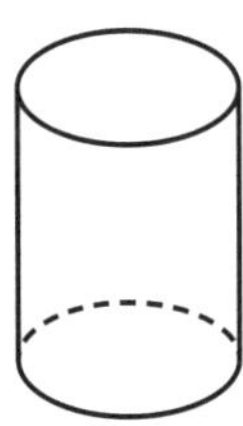
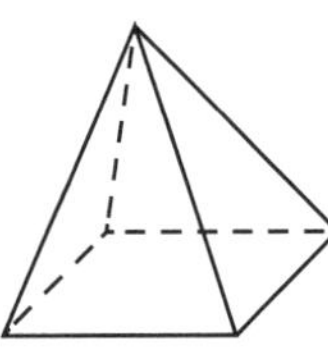

Write their names in the order that they can be stacked.

Bottom ______________________________

Middle ______________________________

Top ______________________________

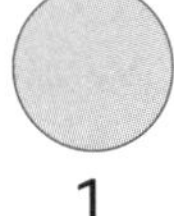

1

Marks

4. Sort the 2D shapes in the correct place on the sorting diagram. Write the letter for each shape.

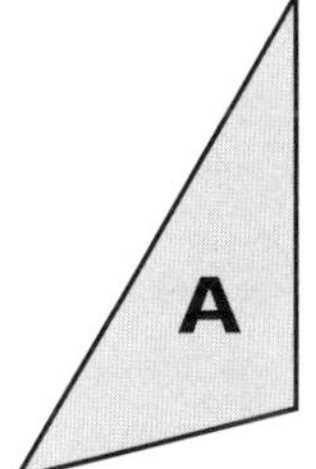

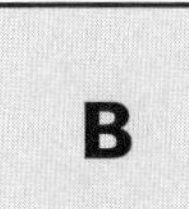

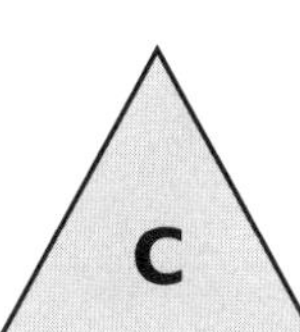

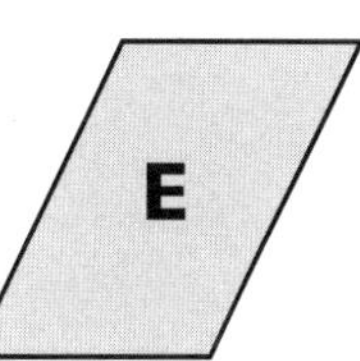

Irregular polygons **Regular polygons**

1

Marks

5. This is part of a multiplication table.
Complete the missing numbers.

<table>
<tr><td></td><td></td><td></td><td>48</td><td></td></tr>
<tr><td></td><td></td><td></td><td>56</td><td></td></tr>
<tr><td>40</td><td>48</td><td></td><td></td><td>72</td></tr>
<tr><td></td><td></td><td></td><td></td><td></td></tr>
<tr><td></td><td></td><td></td><td></td><td></td></tr>
</table>

1

Marks

6. Yolanda has 90p in her pocket.

She lends 30p to her friend, and then buys herself some chocolate for 40p.

On the way home she meets her Grandma, who gives her 20p.

How much money does she have now?

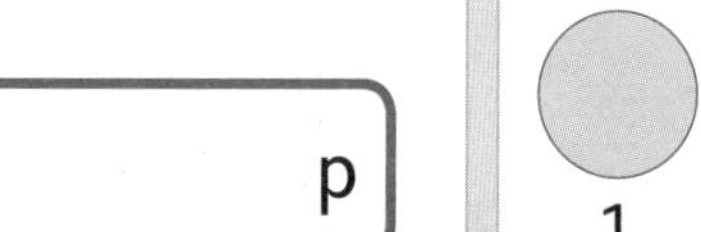

1

Marks

7. On a double-decker bus there are 30 seats downstairs and 40 seats upstairs.

There is also a seat for the driver and room for a few people to stand.

Downstairs, $\frac{1}{3}$ of the seats have passengers in them and upstairs $\frac{1}{2}$ the seats have passengers in them. There is also a driver. How many people are on the bus altogether?

people

1

Well done! END OF SET C TEST 3!

START

Set D

Test 1: Arithmetic

10 MINS

Marks

1. $50 + 50 =$

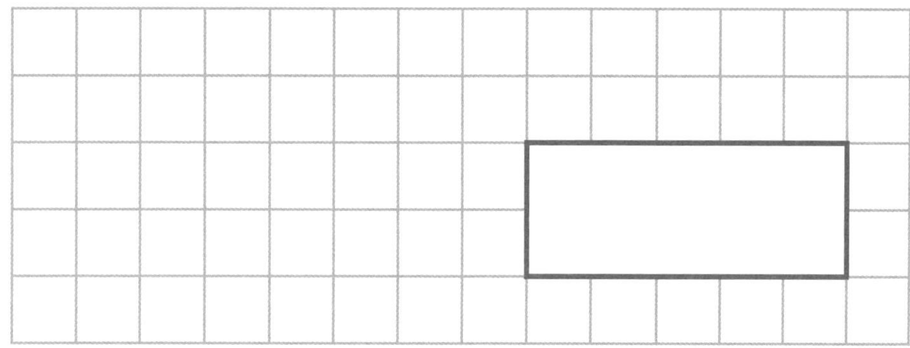

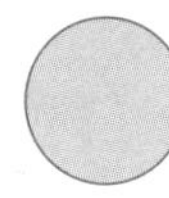

[ ] 1

2. $39 \div 3 =$

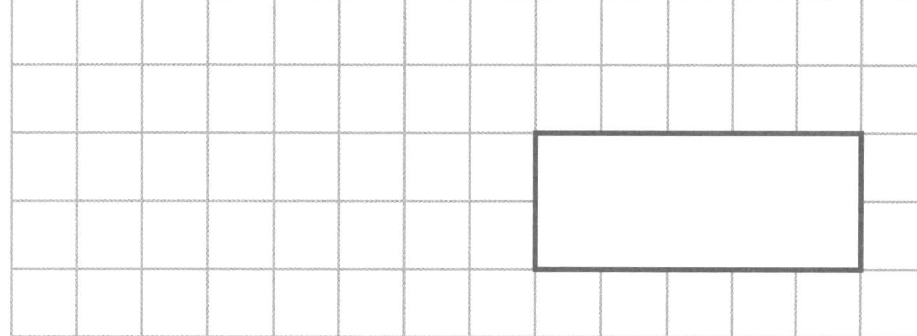

[ ] 1

3. $19 - \square = 12$

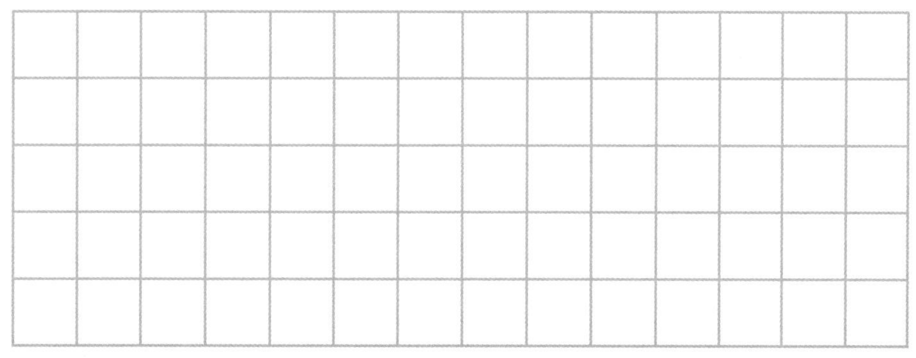

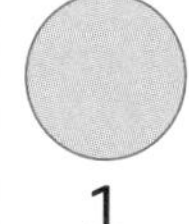

[ ] 1

Marks

4. $9 \times 4 =$

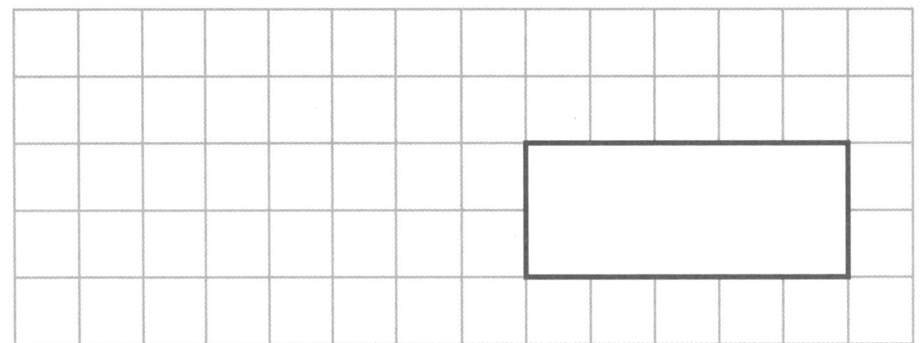

1

5. $405 + 70 =$

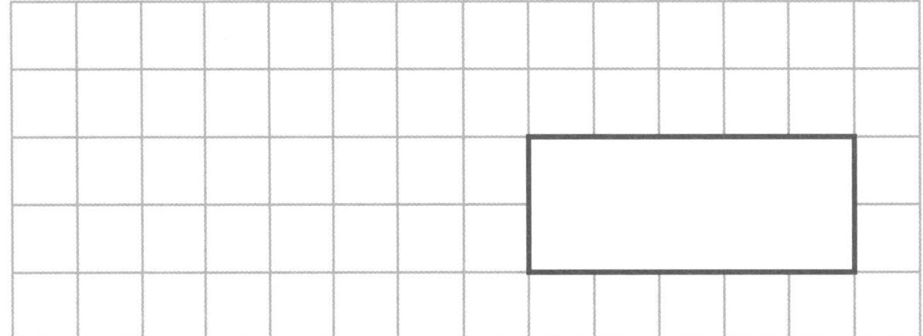

1

6. $\frac{1}{10} + \frac{1}{10} + \frac{1}{10} \quad \frac{1}{10} + \frac{1}{10} + \frac{1}{10} + \frac{1}{10} =$

1

Set D

Test 1: Arithmetic

Marks

7. $5 \times 15 =$

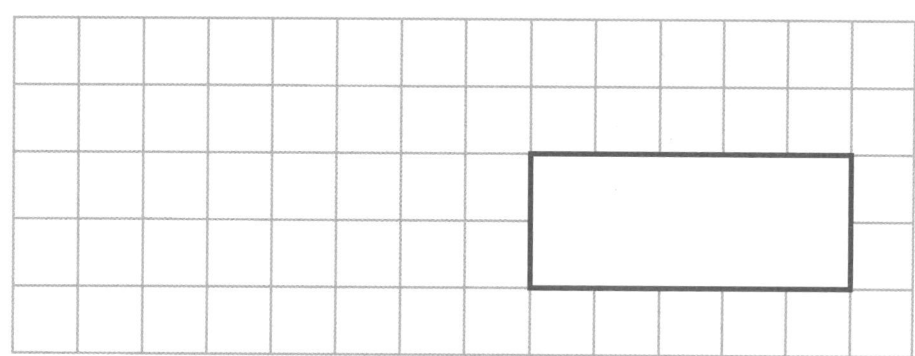

1

8. $365 - 259 =$

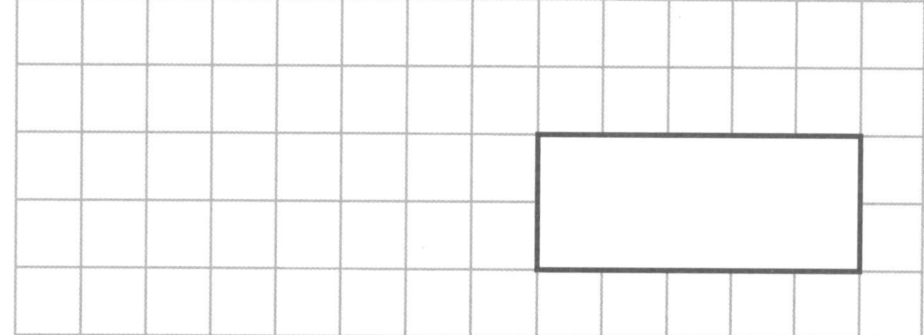

1

9. $\frac{2}{9} + \frac{5}{9} =$

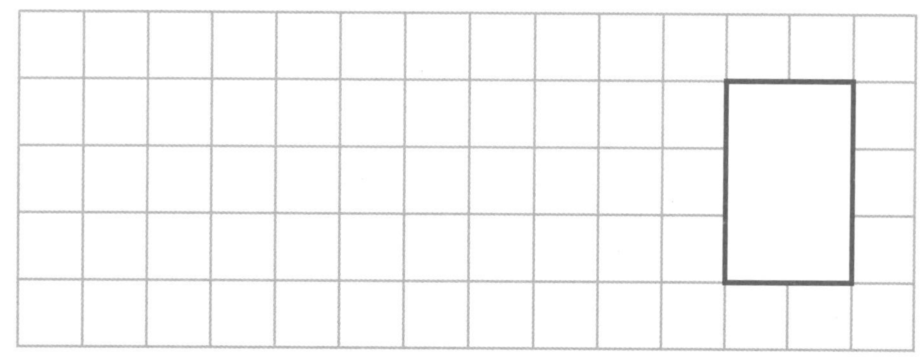

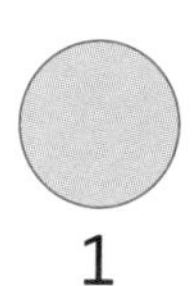

1

Marks

10.

Show your method

$4 \overline{)572}$

2

Well done! END OF SET D TEST 1!

Set D

Test 2: Reasoning

Marks

1. A farmer keeps her sheep in four different fields. There are black sheep and white sheep in each field.

Write the fraction of sheep that are black in each field. One has been done for you.

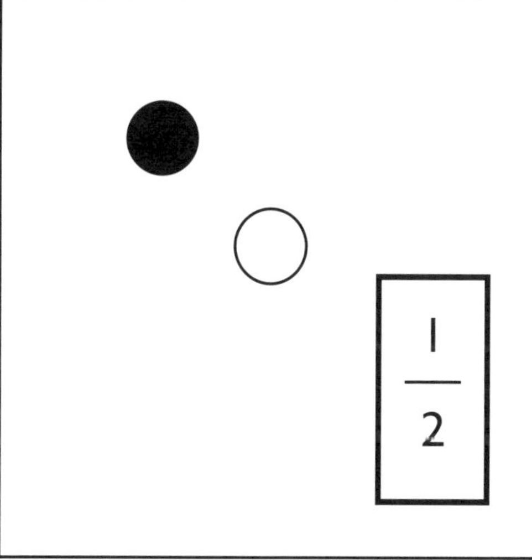

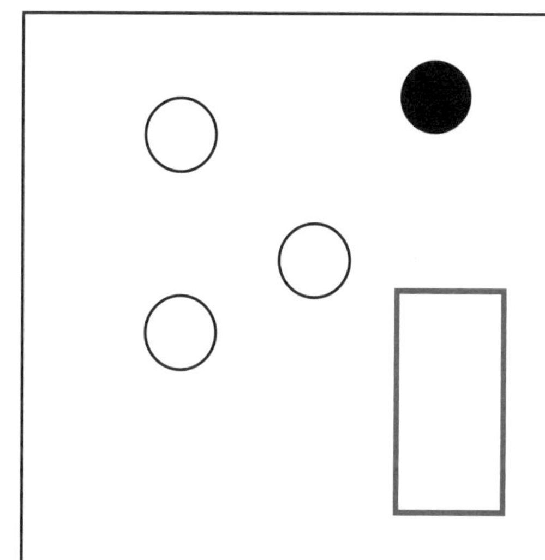

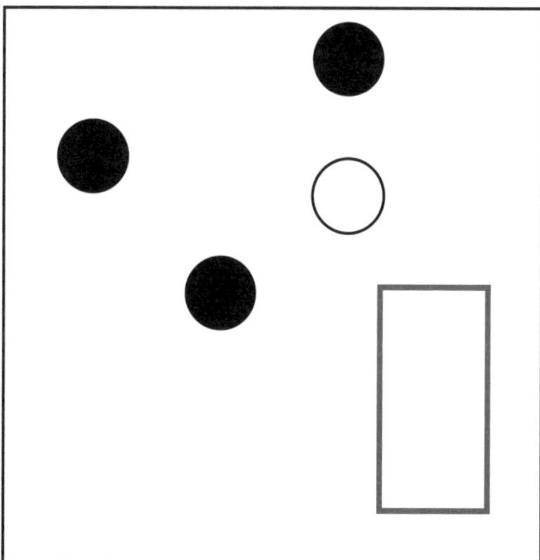

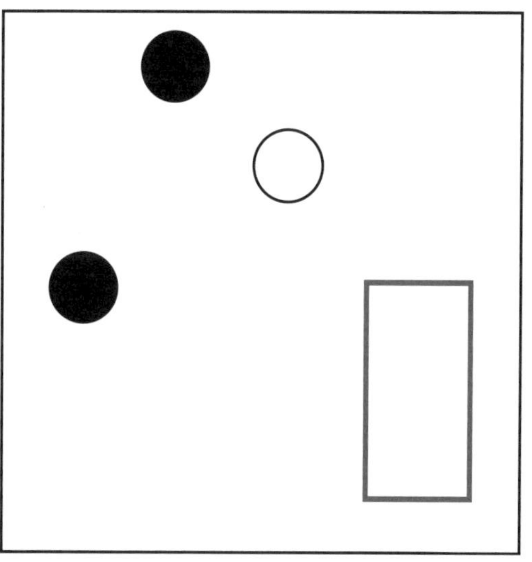

1

Set D

Test 2: Reasoning

2. Put these four numbers into the spaces to make **two** true statements.

791 971 719 179

□ > □

□ < □

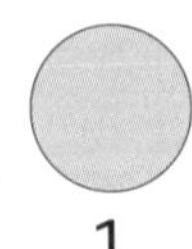

1

Write a *greater than* or a *less than* sign in the space below to make a true statement.

368 □ 371

---

3. Write the missing digits to complete this subtraction.

$$
\begin{array}{r}
4\;\square\;3 \\
-\;\square\;5\;4 \\
\hline
1\;0\;9 \\
\hline
\end{array}
$$

Marks

4. Shane has one of each type of coin in his pocket.
How much money does he have altogether?

1

He buys a figure for 83p and a ball for £3.

How much money will he have left?

1

Angie has a £5 note.

Large stickers cost 50p each.

How many stickers can she buy? stickers

1

Set D

Test 2: Reasoning

Marks

5. In a skyscraper hotel there are 6 rooms on every floor, except for the top two floors, where there are only 3 rooms on each floor.

If the hotel has 84 rooms altogether, how many floors does it have?

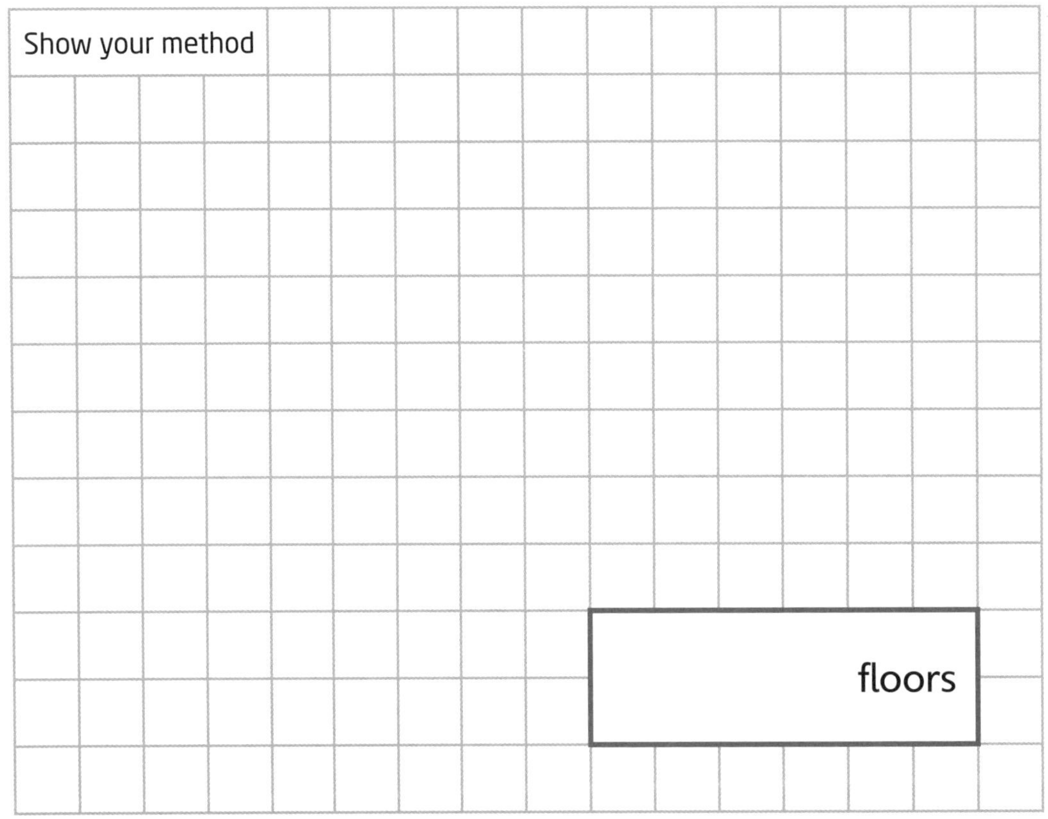

2

Well done! END OF SET D TEST 2!

Set D

Test 3: Reasoning

Marks

1. How many right-angles does this arrow need to turn to point straight up the page?

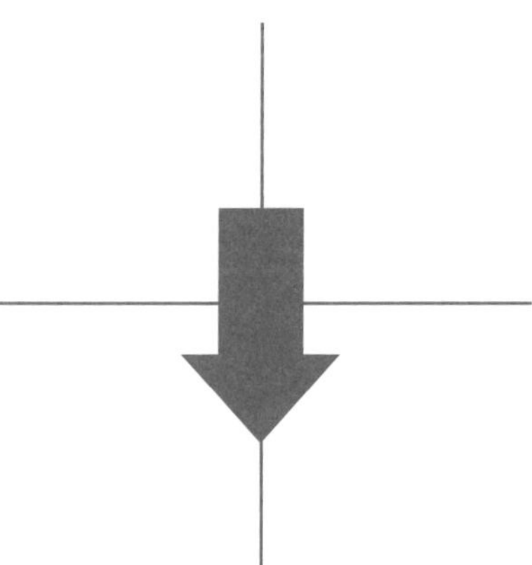

right-angles

1

2. A new box of cornflakes has 600g of cereal inside.

George and his friends eat one third of the cornflakes.

How many grams of cornflakes are left over?

g

1

Marks

3. A school offers three lunch options each day: hot dinner, sandwiches or jacket potato. The table shows the number of children who had each option each day of the week.

	Monday	Tuesday	Wednesday	Thursday	Friday
Hot dinner	47	42	51	38	42
Sandwiches	18	12	6	20	16
Jacket potato	36	47	44	43	43

For the whole week, how many more children had a hot dinner than children had a jacket potato?

Show your method

children

2

Set D

Test 3: Reasoning

Marks

4. There are three different problems below, each with one missing digit.

Use each of these three digits **once** to solve the problems.

4 6 8

18, 15, 12, 9, ☐, 3, 0

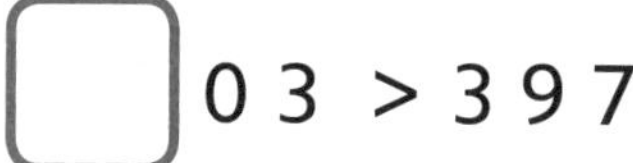

Five hundred and eighty-six = 5☐6

1

---

5. Write the missing digits to make this division correct.

2 4 5

1

Marks

6. A school caretaker uses white paint to paint a grid of 4 rectangles on the school field.

Each rectangle is 4m wide and 6m high.

WHITE

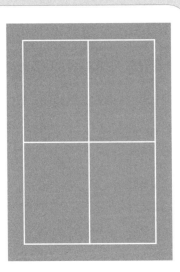

If one tin of paint can make 10m of white line, how many tins of paint will be needed altogether?

Show your method

tins

2

Well done! END OF SET D TEST 3!

Answers

Maths

Q	Mark scheme for Set A Test 1 – Arithmetic	Marks
1	15	1
2	37	1
3	$\frac{4}{10}$	1
4	50	1
5	400	1
6	$\frac{1}{5}$	1
7	611	1
8	8	1
9	436	1
10	762 **Award 1 mark** for a correct method but with one arithmetical error.	2
	Total	**11**

Q	Mark scheme for Set A Test 2 – Reasoning	Marks
1	62 – sixty-two 145 – **one hundred and forty-five** **683** – six hundred and eighty-three 904 – **nine hundred and four**	1
2	50p, 90p, 70p	1
3	950	1
4	**a.** Rhombus Do not accept parallelogram or quadrilateral. **b.** Rectangle. Do not accept oblong or quadrilateral. Wording may vary, but description must include the following facts: four right-angles or four equal angles; two pairs of equal sides that are parallel.	1 1
5	He will receive 2 pounds and 50 pence change. Answers may vary but check total is correct. For example, two pound coins and 50p coin circled.	1 1
6	83 stickers **Award 1 mark** for working which shows a suitable approach to solving the problem but with a maximum of one arithmetical error.	2
	Total	**9**

Q	Mark scheme for Set A Test 3 – Reasoning	Marks
1	Answers may vary. 4 beads should be circled – this can be as one group, individually or otherwise.	1
2	Lunch starts at 12.30pm; Alonso gets home at 4.15pm. Only award mark if both answers are correct. clock hands should be unambiguous, and times indicated accurate to within 2mm.	1
3	Rectangle should be 12cm by 4 cm, with all sides accurate to within 2mm. 32cm	1 1
4	Accept counting in steps of 110, or add 110 each time.	1
5	2 squares each	1
6	5 hours Monday and Wednesday	1 1
	Total	**8**

Q	Mark scheme for Set B Test 1 – Arithmetic	Marks
1	$\frac{3}{10}$	1
2	36	1
3	20	1
4	6	1
5	105	1
6	459	1
7	$\frac{6}{7}$	1
8	20	1
9	414	1
10	912 **Award 1 mark** for a correct method but with one arithmetical error.	2
	Total	**11**

Q	Mark scheme for Set B Test 2 – Reasoning	Marks
1	(see table below)	1
2	0, $\frac{1}{5}$, $\frac{1}{3}$, $\frac{1}{2}$, $\frac{3}{4}$, 1	1

Rounded to the nearest 10	Number	Rounded to the nearest 100
410	412	400
290	287	**300**
650	647	**600**

Q	Mark scheme for Set B Test 2 – Reasoning	Marks
3	Only award mark if the missing sides have been drawn accurately, to within 2mm Hexagon	1 1
4	375 add 159 equals 534 OR 159 add 375 equals 534 OR 375 + 159 = 534 OR 159 + 375 = 534	1
5	7 more books Note that there is more than one way to find the answer. **Award 1 mark** for working which shows a suitable approach to solving the problem but with a maximum of one arithmetical error.	2
6	120ml **Award 1 mark** for working which shows a suitable approach to solving the problem but with a maximum of one arithmetical error.	2
	Total	**9**

Q	Mark scheme for Set B Test 3 – Reasoning	Marks
1	$\frac{1}{12}$ – 1 cross, for example $\frac{1}{3}$ – 4 crosses, for example $\frac{1}{4}$ – 3 crosses, for example Crosses can be in any seats. Only award mark if all three are unambiguously correct.	1
2	6 3 **7** + 1 **8** 4 8 2 1	1
3	Accept 3 and a half hours or 3 hours and 30 minutes. 15 minutes	1 1
4	**Award 1 mark** for: parallel line, perpendicular line, vertical line **A** Right-angle **B** Acute angle **C** Obtuse angle **D** Right-angle	1 1
5	70 children **Award 1 mark** for working which shows a suitable approach to solving the problem but with a maximum of one arithmetical error.	2
	Total	**8**

Q	Mark scheme for Set C Test 1 – Arithmetic	Marks
1	4	1
2	700	1
3	20	1
4	$\frac{3}{10}$	1
5	6	1
6	105	1
7	$\frac{3}{8}$	1
8	360	1
9	929	1
10	42 **Award 1 mark** for a correct method but with one arithmetical error.	2
	Total	**11**

Q	Mark scheme for Set C Test 2 – Reasoning	Marks
1	5cm	1
2	**2** 6 × 3 7 **8**	1
3	2, **5**, **8**, **11**	1
4	$\frac{1}{3}$. Accept $\frac{3}{9}$.	1
5	£30 £5 £4	1 1 1
6	Least popular: <u>Zebra</u> Most popular: <u>Elephant</u> 4 children	1 1
	Total	**9**

Q	Mark scheme for Set C Test 3 – Reasoning	Marks
1	284 OR 428 OR 482 OR 824	1
2	3kg 79kg	1 1
3	Bottom: <u>cuboid</u> OR <u>cylinder</u> Middle: <u>cylinder</u> OR <u>cuboid</u> Top: <u>square-based pyramid</u>	1
4	**Irregular polygons**: A, D, E **Regular polygons**: B, C	1

Q	Mark scheme for Set C Test 3 – Reasoning	Marks
5	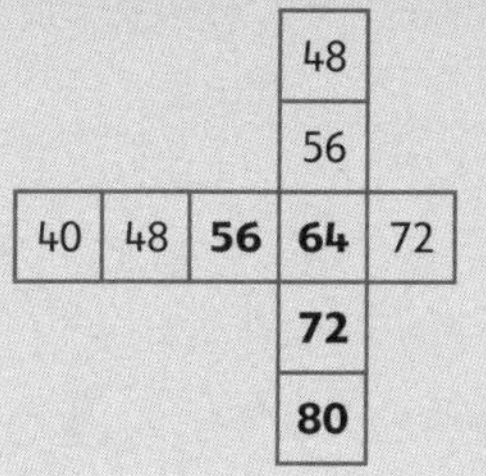 Vertical column: 48, 56, **64**, **72**, **80**; horizontal row: 40, 48, **56**, **64**, 72	1
6	40p	1
7	31 people	1
	Total	**8**

Q	Mark scheme for Set D Test 1 – Arithmetic	Marks
1	100	1
2	13	1
3	7	1
4	36	1
5	475	1
6	$\frac{7}{10}$	1
7	75	1
8	106	1
9	$\frac{7}{9}$	1
10	143 **Award 1 mark** for a correct method but with one arithmetical error.	2
	Total	**11**

Q	Mark scheme for Set D Test 2 – Reasoning	Marks
1	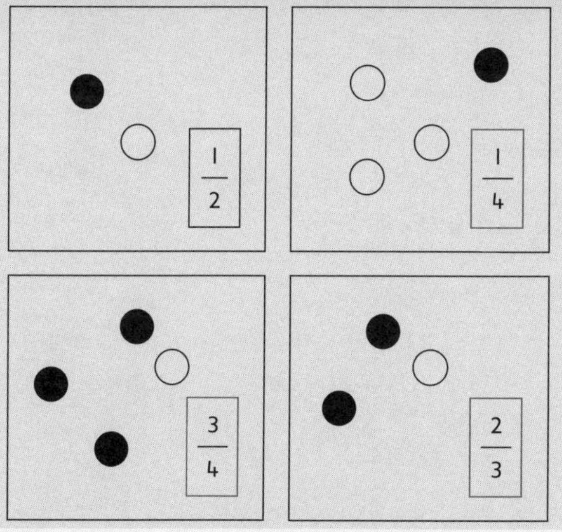 Four boxes: 1 black, 1 white counter – $\frac{1}{2}$; 1 black, 3 white counters – $\frac{1}{4}$; 3 black, 1 white counter – $\frac{3}{4}$; 2 black, 1 white counter – $\frac{2}{3}$	1
2	Various answers are possible. Ensure that both statements are true. For example, **971** > **179**; **719** < **791**. 368 (<) 371	1 1

Q	Mark scheme for Set D Test 2 – Reasoning	Marks
3	4 (6) 3 − (3) 5 4 1 0 9	1
4	Accept £3.88; £3 and 88p; or the answer in words with near-accurate spelling. Accept 5p or the answer in words with near-accurate spelling. 10 stickers	1 1 1
5	15 floors **Award 1 mark** for working which shows a suitable approach to solving the problem but with a maximum of one arithmetical error.	2
	Total	**9**

Q	Mark scheme for Set D Test 3 – Reasoning	Marks
1	2 right-angles	1
2	400g	1
3	7 children **Award 1 mark** for working which shows a suitable approach to solving the problem but with a maximum of one arithmetical error.	2
4	18 15 12 9 (6) 3 0 (4)03 > 397 Five hundred and eighty-six = 5(8)6	1
5	2 4 5 3 ⟌ (7) 3 (5)	1
6	6 tins **Award 1 mark** for working which shows a suitable approach to solving the problem but with a maximum of one arithmetical error.	2
	Total	**8**

Skills check

Maths

General notes for parents and teachers:

- In the National Curriculum tests, approximately 85% of marks are from the Place Value, Addition and Subtraction, Multiplication and Division, Fractions, Ratio and proportion and Algebra content areas.
- Where a statement below indicates that the skill should be completed mentally, rough jottings are acceptable.

Number – Number and place value

I can count from 0 in multiples of 4, 8, 50 and 100; find 10 or 100 more or less than a given number, for example, 0, 50, 100, 150...

I can recognise the place value of each digit in a three-digit number (hundreds, tens, ones), for example, the 5 in 358 is worth 50.

I can compare and order numbers up to 1000, for example, 649 < 712.

I can identify, represent and estimate numbers using different representations, for example, numbers as measures: the table is 127cm long.

I can read and write numbers up to 1000 in numerals and in words, for example, eight hundred and forty-seven is 847.

I can solve number problems and practical problems involving these ideas, for example, two tables joined together will be 254cm long.

Number – addition and subtraction

I can add and subtract numbers mentally, including:

- a three-digit number and ones, for example, 345 + 8 = 353
- a three-digit number and tens, for example, 278 + 30 = 308
- a three-digit number and hundreds, for example, 507 + 400 = 907

I can add and subtract numbers with up to three digits, using formal written methods of columnar addition and subtraction, for example,

$$\begin{array}{r} 5\ 6\ 2 \\ +\ 3\ 5\ 7 \\ \hline 9\ 1\ 9 \\ \hline {\scriptstyle 1} \end{array}$$

I can estimate the answer to a calculation and use inverse operations to check answers, for example, 562 + 357 is approximately 900. Also, 919 – 562 = 357 so the above addition must be correct.

I can solve problems, including missing number problems, using number facts, place value, and more complex addition and subtraction, for example, 432 out of 620 children are girls, so 620 − 432 = 188 must be boys.

Skills check

Maths

Number – multiplication and division

I can recall and use multiplication and division facts for the 2, 5, 10, 3, 4 and 8 multiplication tables, for example, $9 \times 8 = 72$.

I can write and calculate mathematical statements for multiplication and division using the multiplication tables that I know, including for two-digit numbers times one-digit numbers, using mental and progressing to formal written methods, for example,

$$\begin{array}{r} 2\ 3 \\ \times \quad 5 \\ \hline 1\ 1\ 5 \\ \hline {}_{1}\ \ \end{array}$$

I can solve problems, including missing number problems, involving multiplication and division, including positive integer scaling problems and correspondence problems in which *n* objects are connected to *m* objects, for example, Tina's mum has twice as many pairs of gloves as she does scarves. If she has 6 scarves how many gloves will she have altogether? ($6 \times 2 = 12$ gloves).

Number – fractions (including decimals)

I can count up and down in tenths; recognise that tenths arise from dividing an object into 10 equal parts and in dividing one-digit numbers or quantities by 10, for example, $\frac{1}{10} + \frac{1}{10} + \frac{1}{10} = \frac{3}{10}$.

I can recognise, find and write fractions of a discrete set of objects: unit fractions and non-unit fractions with small denominators, for example, circle $\frac{1}{2}$ of these 10 bricks (5 are circled).

I can recognise and use fractions as numbers: unit fractions and non-unit fractions with small denominators, for example, position simple fractions on a number line.

I can recognise and show, using diagrams, equivalent fractions with small denominators, for example, show that five out of ten circled objects are equivalent to half a shaded circle.

I can add and subtract fractions with the same denominator within one whole, for example, $\frac{5}{7} + \frac{1}{7} = \frac{6}{7}$.

I can compare and order unit fractions and fractions with the same denominators, for example, $\frac{5}{8} > \frac{3}{8}$.

I can solve problems that involve all of the above, for example, $\frac{1}{2}$ of 10 pencils (5) is more than a quarter of 16 pencils (4).

Measurement

I can measure, compare, add and subtract: lengths (m/cm/mm); mass (kg/g); volume/capacity (l/ml), for example, a 47cm stick is longer than a 39cm stone.

Skills check

Maths

I can measure the perimeter of simple 2D shapes, for example, the perimeter of a rectangle is 12cm, measured with a ruler.

I can add and subtract amounts of money to give change, using both £ and p in practical contexts, for example, If I buy a comic for £2 and a toy for 50p, with a £5 note, I will get £2 and 50p change (note – decimal notation is not expected in Year 3).

I can tell and write the time from an analogue clock, including using Roman numerals from I to XII, and 12-hour and 24-hour clocks, for example, 3pm is 15:00.

I can estimate and read time with increasing accuracy to the nearest minute; record and compare time in terms of seconds, minutes and hours; use vocabulary such as o'clock, am/pm, morning, afternoon, noon and midnight, for example, the television programme will finish two minutes before noon.

I know the number of seconds in a minute and the number of days in each month, year and leap year, for example, there are 366 days in a leap year.

I can compare durations of events, for example, to calculate the time taken by particular events or tasks.

Geometry – properties of shape

I can draw 2D shapes and make 3D shapes using modelling materials; recognise 3D shapes in different orientations and describe them, for example, a cube has six square faces.

I can recognise angles as a property of shape or a description of a turn, for example, a square has a right angle in each corner.

I can identify right angles, recognise that two right angles make a half-turn, three make three quarters of a turn and four a complete turn; identify whether angles are greater than or less than a right angle, for example, the robot has turned more than one right-angle, but less than two right-angles.

I can identify horizontal and vertical lines and pairs of perpendicular and parallel lines, for example, a rectangle has two pairs of parallel lines for its sides, and these pairs are perpendicular.

Statistics

I can interpret and present data using bar charts, pictograms and tables, for example, use a pictogram to find which is the most popular pet.

I can solve one-step and two-step questions using information presented in scaled bar charts, pictograms and tables, for example, 'How many more dogs are there than cats?' and 'How many fewer guinea pigs are there than cats?'

Progress chart

Fill in your score in the table below to see how well you've done.

	Score
Set A Test 1	
Set A Test 2	
Set A Test 3	
Set B Test 1	
Set B Test 2	
Set B Test 3	
Set C Test 1	
Set C Test 2	
Set C Test 3	
Set D Test 1	
Set D Test 2	
Set D Test 3	
TOTAL	

Mark	
0–38	Good try! You need more practice in some topics – ask an adult to help you.
39–79	You're doing really well. Ask for extra help for any topics you found tricky.
80–112	You're a 10-Minute SATs Test maths star – good work!

You have completed all of the 10-Minute SATs Tests

Name: ______________________

Date: ______________________